YOU ARE UNDER ATTACK

SEVEN WAYS TO DEFEAT THE ENEMY

SABRINA D. THORPS

DREAMWISE PUBLISHING
Columbus, GA
A Dreamwise Company

All Scripture quotations, unless otherwise indicated, are taken from the King James Version of the Bible.

Scripture quotations marked AMP are taken from the Amplified Bible, Copyright 1954, 1958, 1962, 1964, 1965, 1987, 2015 by The Lockman Foundation. All rights reserved. Used by permission. (www.Lockman.org)

YOU ARE UNDER ATTACK

Copyright © 2021 by Sabrina D. Thorps.

All rights reserved. Printed in the United States of America. No part of this book may be used or reproduced in any manner whatsoever without written permission from the Publisher.

For information contact :

Dreamwise Publishing

Columbus, GA 31907

http://www.dreamwisepublishing.com

Cover design by Dreamwise Web Solutions

Cover photo 1 by McAdams (Adobe Stock Photos)

Cover photo 2 by Pete Will (Getty Images)

Author Photo by Carmen Buckner Photography

ISBN: 978-1-737-0555-0-1 (Paperback)

ISBN: 978-1-737-0555-1-8 (E-Book)

Limits of Liability and Disclaimer :

The author and Publisher shall not be liable for misuse of this material. This book is strictly for educational and informational purposes.

Dedication

I dedicate this book to my parents, who have been a sure example of God's strength in my life. Thank you, mom, and dad, for teaching me that even when losing the natural battle, we can still win the spiritual war. I love you both. RIP Daddy.

~Love Sabrina

Contents

Introduction 10

Under Attack 16

Indicators of Under Attack 21

Seven Ways to Defeat the Enemy 35

    I. Gird Up Your Loins With Truth 41

    II. Put on the Breastplate of Righteousness 45

    III. Shod Your Feet With the Gospel of Peace 49

    IV. Lift Up the Shield of Faith 52

    V. Take the Helmet of Salvation 57

    VI. Take the Sword of the Spirit 61

    VII. Pray 66

Conclusion 72

Prayer of Thanksgiving 74

About the Author 77

Acknowledgments

All Glory, Honor, and Praise go to my God, my Lord, and Savior Jesus Christ. Lord, I THANK YOU for EVERYTHING! You have been my guide, my teacher, my counselor, my rock, my strength, my joy, my crown, my hope of Glory, and the center of my life. You have made everything that was impossible for me possible!

To Jashawn & Jaishira: You are the reasons why I fight. Thank you for trusting in me as your Mother. I love you both more than your little hearts could ever imagine.

To Byron: Thank you for being a wonderful dad, co-parent, and friend. I appreciate all that you do.

To Contrillio Thank you for being my sister, my friend, my top reader, and for encouraging me in everything I do. I appreciate how you have encouraged me to write.

To Conzonia: Thank you for being my encourager and for all the things you have done for me. I cannot count the cost.

To Patricia, Polly, Roxie, Cynthia, & Darron: Thank you all for everything. I could not have asked for better siblings. RIP Buddy

To My Nieces & Nephews: Thanks for always making me feel like a special Auntie. You guys are near and dear to my heart. Stay strong and stay encouraged.

To Samantha, Tekila & Families: Thank you for being my best friends for over 23 years. Thank you for being friends I can talk to and my go-to place to vent. Words cannot express my gratitude.

To Apostle Abernathy & TVM Family: Thank you for everything. I appreciate all your prayers, teachings, encouragement, and support.

To: Apostle Acklin, Apostle Stallworth, & Pastor Worthy: Thank you for your great leadership and the Word of God you poured into my life.

To Daddy Ted: Thank you for your daily encouragement and for loving me as your daughter. I will forever be grateful.

To Archbishop Toney, Apostle Dee, & Elect Lady Daisy: Thank you for your love, encouragement, and for trusting the God in me.

To My Extended Family, Friends & Loved Ones: Thank you. I love you all!

Introduction

"For though we walk in the flesh, we do not war after the flesh. For the weapons of our warfare are not carnal, but mighty through God to the pulling down of strongholds."
~2 Corinthians 10:3-4

Have you ever felt as if the whole world was on your shoulders and that everything, and everyone, was all coming down on you at the same time? Do you feel beaten up or beaten down, yet to realize that no one is physically putting their hands on you? Do you feel as if every time you turn around, something or someone is coming against you? Do you feel let down, tired, discouraged, confused, and left to deal with it all on your own? Do you feel abandoned? Are you suddenly questioning your call to the ministry or questioning the identity of who you are in God? Do you feel like giving up, throwing in the towel, and just walking away from it all?

If you answered yes to any of these questions, then, most likely, you are Under Attack. You are or have been, experiencing what most Christians refer to as *Spiritual Warfare.* Whenever you connect with God or have anything to do with God, you will always be a huge candidate for Spiritual Warfare.

According to Wikipedia.org, Spiritual Warfare is the Christian concept of fighting against the work of preternatural evil forces. It is based on the biblical belief in evil spirits, or demons, that are said to intervene in human affairs in various ways. According to Merriam-Webster.com, warfare, on the other hand, are military operations between enemies.

Satan is and has always been, an enemy of God,

even from the beginning of time. It started when God cast him down out of Heaven into darkness and he, Satan, has been warring with God ever since. This spiritual battle between good and evil, God and Satan, starts in the spiritual realm and, sometimes, manifests in the natural realm. Therefore, affecting one's life in areas of mental stability, health, careers, dreams, goals, finances, families, relationships, and marriages. If not dealt with early on, it can lead to mental instability, emotional trauma, depression, thoughts of suicide, and more.

Look around you. I am sure you can see some of these manifestations in the natural. There are people killing people. People giving up, quitting, and even taking their own lives. The world we live in is in trouble and many of God's people are in spiritual chaos. Have you ever wondered where all of it is coming from?

The majority of what we face in life comes from Spiritual Warfare. We are in a battle in this world, and it is not always a natural battle that we can see with the naked eye. Neither is it always a physical battle that we can feel with our natural hands. Often, we find ourselves in a spiritual battle; one that we may not see and may not even know is there, but it exists. It is real.

The enemy takes pleasure in starting our days, weeks, months, and even years off with discouragement. He wants to keep us in defeat, fear, worry, stress, and anxiety. If you are a child of God or a follower of Jesus Christ, you are one of the first he tries to attack. At some point in your spiritual journey, you will encounter attacks and you will experience spiritual warfare.

God reminds us daily, in His Word, to fear not. If you read from Genesis to Revelation in the Holy Bible, you will encounter those words at least 365 times. That is once for each day of the week for 365 days of the year. Each morning, when you get out of bed, you should always look in the mirror and remind yourself to "Fear Not."

God also tells us, in His Word, to stay alert of Satan's schemes and to always watch and pray. For us to do this, we must obey His words and walk closely with Him. He has given us strategies and instructions that we must follow to stand against Satan and his threats. We must clothe ourselves in God's garments of protection and arm ourselves with His spiritual weapons. Not only should we clothe ourselves in His garments of protection, but we must also seek Him for guidance every day of our lives. God desires to teach us, train us, and guide us but we must move closer to Him by spending time with Him through prayer, praise, and worship.

As you continue to grow in God and learn who He truly is, He will equip you with the wisdom, knowledge, and strength to stand against the evil forces of this world in the powerful name of Jesus. You will never have to fight this battle alone because God says, in His Word, that He will never leave you nor forsake you. Even when you cannot see that He is there fighting for you, believe that He is. He will send you a reminder to let you know that He is always with you.

So, my desire for this book is to encourage you while you are in the battle, and my purpose for this book is to inform and to educate. I will give you four indicators to look for when you are under attack and how to combat them. I will also point out seven ways, from the Bible, that God has given us to overcome these attacks. If we follow these seven ways, then we have hope that the battle is already won, the enemy is already defeated, and the victory is already ours!

"Victory is given to those who will reach up and grab it. God has already made victory possible, so it is up to us to reach up and grab it."
~Sabrina D. Thorps

Under Attack

"For we wrestle not against flesh and blood, but against principalities, against powers, against the rulers of the darkness of this world, against spiritual wickedness in high places."
~Ephesians 6:12

I remember a time when I found myself experiencing spiritual warfare to the tenth power. I stumbled across a conversation that I, on the other hand, was not a part of. Although I was not a part of it, I felt as if I could have very well been on the topic for discussion. At the time, this was not the only thing I had been going through, but it was enough to push me out on the battlefield.

Suddenly, I began to feel as if knives were being thrown at me and I was getting stabbed by everyone. I started feeling some type of way and I began to question God and who He had called me to be. I found myself, inwardly, replaying things in my head and wondering how I had gotten to this place in my life. For a moment, I felt as if I was set up by God and dropped off by the side of the road. This feeling went on for days, then weeks and I had no idea why this was happening to me.

Then, one day, I heard God speak so clearly the words in my ear "*You Are Under Attack.*" When I heard this, it was like my spirit man woke up. A light had come on. So, I immediately went into prayer and God began to download in me an understanding of what was really going on. He even showed me things in a dream to reveal to me what I could not see with the naked eye. He showed me, in the dream, the faces of two people in the act of practicing witchcraft on me. One practiced it while the other one assisted. I remember telling this person, in the dream, that it would not work. My first thought, when I woke up, was there was no way this could be true.

These were the faces of Christian leaders in God's Kingdom. So, I decided not to dwell on it long.

After that, maybe a few weeks later, I came home one day to only find that my mailbox had been shattered with bird feathers and blood. The foot of the bird was standing so straight up and neat in the door handle of my mailbox that it looked as if someone had been placed there. I lived at the end of a cul-de-sac and there was no way a car could have gotten enough speed to go fast enough to shatter a bird like that.

I knew, then, what I was dealing with, and I was not afraid. I knew, then, that what I was going through, and the type of enemy I was facing, could not be seen with the naked eye. I was in a battle that could not be seen, and I knew I had to fight an invisible enemy with supernatural weapons. I knew I was in *Spiritual Warfare* and had come face-to-face with an enemy that could only be dealt with in the spiritual realm. My first reaction was to pray.

So, I later called my Pastor and I told him of the things I had been experiencing and the dream I had. Of course, He covered me in prayer and told me ways I could deal with it. I listened. At first, I had no idea what was happening in my life when it all began. Yes, I had experienced some warfare in my past, but I did not understand what it was at the time. It was by the grace of God that I made it through those times, not knowing why certain things were going on in my life. This time was the first time that I had been introduced to Spiritual Warfare, on such a level, and finally understood what it was.

Sometimes, we can experience things in our lives and not know exactly what it is or where it is coming from. Our issue is not always the fact that we are under attack, but it is when we fail to *recognize when* we are under attack.

So, in these next chapters, you will find four main indicators that will help you recognize when you are under attack and how to combat them. You will also find, in these next chapters, seven ways to defeat the enemy.

You may wonder why only four indicators when there are many indicators, and why only seven ways when there are many ways? Deuteronomy 28:7 says, "The Lord shall cause thine enemies that rise up against thee to be smitten (defeated) before thy face; they shall come out against thee one way and flee before thee seven ways." In other words, the enemy may come to attack you in one specific way, but God will cause him to flee from you in seven different ways. For example, God can cause him to flee by making him 1) Leave you alone; 2) Turn you loose; 3) Dismiss himself from your presence; 4) Give you back everything he stole from you; 5) Pay you back with interest; 6) Give you double for your trouble; 7) Apologize. Genesis 50:20a says, "But as for you, ye thought evil against me, but God meant it unto good."

"Never fight fear with fear, but always fight fear with faith."
~Sabrina D. Thorps

Indicators of Under Attack

"There hath no temptation taken you, but such is common to man: but God is faithful, who will not suffer you to be tempted above that ye are able; but will with the temptation also make a way to escape, that ye may be able to bear it."
~1 Corinthians 10:13

Whatever we face on earth or in the spiritual realm, God is willing to shed light on it and give us insight. When we pray and ask Him to show us what is hiding behind the scenes, He is willing to bring it to the forefront. He will never allow anything to come against us that our spirit man cannot handle. If we put our trust in Him, He will give us a plan and a way of escape.

One of my *first* indicators to help you recognize when you are under attack is Mental Confusion, or Psychological Warfare. The first place the enemy wants to attack you is in the mind. This is the easiest and quickest way he can reach you and attempt to destroy you, your purpose, and your destiny.

The mind is like a battlefield. In it is much ground for the enemy to play and tread upon. There are so many things that he can do to and with the mind. He is very cunning and very crafty. By the time he is done with the mind, you may be left in a state of mental confusion. Mental confusion is one of the worst kinds of spiritual warfare. It deals with the psychological domain. The intent is to change or decrease your morale, or spirit, so that you will feel less confident and hopeless. The best way for the enemy to accomplish this is by attacking your thought pattern.

When your mind is under attack, sometimes, you begin to question who you are in God and who it is that

God has called you to be. You begin to question your purpose on the earth and why you were called in the first place. You begin to feel, and think, that no one loves you and no one cares for you. You begin to feel that everyone has turned their backs on you and walked away. My dearly beloved, you are not in this battle alone. The enemy's goal is to create those illusions, in your mind, because he knows that once those seeds are planted in your mind, eventually, they will grow into your heart, and that is where he has been trying to get to all along.

So, your opponent is not always one you can see. Your opponent, in this case, is one you cannot see. Yes, sometimes, your opponent can be you. That is why you always hear the older saints say, "We are our worst enemy." That is true; however, it all points back to our real enemy, Satan. He will try to use your mind against you. Always remember that those negative thoughts are not your thoughts. They are his.

If you read Nehemiah Chapter 4, you will see where the enemy messed with Nehemiah's mind to try to make him question whether he could carry out his God-given assignment. What did Nehemiah do? The bible says he prayed. The best way to combat mental confusion is to nip it in the bud in the beginning. Begin with *Prayer*. Prayer should always be the first thing, the second thing, and the last thing you do whenever your mind is under attack. Always pray.

My *second* indicator to help you recognize when you are under attack is *Physical Threats or Physical Attacks*. If the enemy cannot defeat you in the mind, he will then move to another stage of warfare, your body. This is where Satan wants to put his hands on you but, since he is a spirit, he attacks you in your body. This is where he goes after your physical health so that you can feel physical pain.

If you continue to read Nehemiah Chapter 4, you will also see where His enemies tried to come against him physically. Just because he continued in his assignment, his enemies wanted to physically put their hands on him. The enemy will send threats, or attacks, to your body and can cause all kinds of aches, pain, sicknesses, and diseases.

Have you ever experienced so much pain in your bones and joints that all you could do was scream? Has it ever gotten so bad that you could barely walk, or hardly do the things that God called you to do? Have you ever been so sick that all you could do was just lay in bed and wait for that moment to lift and release you? I have. I remember laying on my back, in my bed, looking up and waiting for those moments of attacks to be over. Two of my greatest thoughts were "Lord, when you get me through this one," and "Lord when I ever get up from here."

The enemy's goal is to keep us down so that we cannot preach that message God has placed in our hearts. He does not want you to reach those people God assigned to you to help save, deliver, and set free. Think it not strange when the doctor says, "I've never seen this before," or "There's absolutely nothing we can do about it at this point." Think it not strange when the only one you have left to turn to is God. You must recognize when your body, or health, is under attack and confront the enemy. We must stop accepting every pain and every bad report and reverse it.

When Nehemiah's enemies wanted to attack him physically, what did he do? The bible says that Nehemiah prayed again. So, the way to combat physical threats or physical attacks is with *more prayer*. This is where you must intensify your prayer life. This is where you must get profoundly serious about this battle you are in and pray even more. I am not saying do not seek medical attention or follow your doctor's advice. Do that. What I am saying is to also recognize when it is a physical attack of the enemy and make sure that you pray.

Hannah was barren in her body and the enemy used it as a weapon to attack her. However, Hannah did not go down without a fight. She reversed the curse through prayer. The Bible says, in 1 Samuel 2:1, "Hannah prayed, and said, My heart rejoiceth in the Lord, mine horn(strength) is exalted in the Lord: my mouth is enlarged (opened wide to speak boldly) over mine enemies; because I rejoice in thy salvation." Whenever the enemy intensifies his attacks on your body, you must also intensify your counterattacks in the way you pray.

***

My *third* indicator to help you recognize when you are under attack is *Spiritual Weakness*. A lot of times, the enemy tries to attack the inner man, the spirit man, by wearing you out completely. He has attacked your mind, your body, and now he is ready to attack your spirit man; the very make-up of your entire being.

Spiritual Weakness is somewhat different from physical weakness. Once your body has been healed from the sickness and pain, there is no stopping you now. Therefore, the enemy must go after the spirit man. Have you ever been weak and tired for no reason at all? You did not know why you were tired; you were tired. Tired of going through this and tired of going through that.

I am sure there are times when you felt like you could not make it. You felt like you wanted to give up, give in and give out. Even now, you feel like you just want to throw in the towel and call it quits, sometimes. If you do that, you are doing just what the enemy wants you to do and you are walking away from your true destiny. All the devil wants is for you to forfeit your destiny so that you will not 1) answer the call of God on your life; 2) complete your assignment on the earth, and 3) accomplish the mission that God sent you here to do.

People of God, we cannot give up in this fight. Trials are going to come. Life is going to happen, especially if you are connected to God. It is just like being in a boxing ring. When your opponent beats you down, you have little to no strength left to get up and fight back. All you can do is focus on how weak you are and how strong the attacks are over your life. You can hear the referee counting down and, if you do not get up now, your time may very well be running out. You must get up and fight back. Before you let the devil win, remember that God is in your corner. Jesus is the referee, and the Holy Spirit is your coach. God will never allow the enemy to put more on you than you can bear. If he allows it, then you can bear it. He will never let him cheat you. He is right there, rooting for you and watching over the whole thing.

The Bible says in 2 Corinthians 12:9-10 "And He said unto me, My grace is sufficient for thee: for my strength is made perfect in weakness. Most gladly therefore will I rather glory in my infirmities, that the power of Christ may rest upon me. Therefore, I take pleasure in infirmities, in reproaches, in necessities, in persecutions, in distresses for Christ's sake: for when I am weak, then am I strong. It is in your most trying times and weakest moments that you will see the Power of God. This is the time where you will see that God is mighty and strong. This is the time when He wants you to turn it all over to Him so that He can show you His wondrous working power.

As you begin to see Him fighting on your behalf and working things out in your favor, a strength will rise in you so great and so strong that you cannot help but jump up with praise. In Judges Chapter 1, the children of Israel asked the Lord who shall go up for us against the Canaanites first, to fight against them? The Lord answered and said "Judah shall go up: behold, I have delivered the land into his hand. Well, Judah means praise. You must march forward with praise.

When you see God's true love for you, you cannot help but give Him Glory. You cannot help but to praise Him for His faithfulness; praise Him for His grace; praise Him for His mercy and praise Him for His lovingkindness toward you. This will give you strength like none other. So, the way to combat spiritual weakness is with *Praise*.

My *fourth* indicator to help you recognize when you are under attack is *Fear and Anxiety*. By now, the enemy knows that you are not so easily defeated. He now knows that you are a tough one to handle. This is where he must bring out his big dawgs (more demons, more spirits, more illusions.) This is where he tries to instill so much fear and anxiety in you, thus causing you to be afraid, worry, and stress. At this point, he wants you to stress yourself completely out. Did you know that stress and anxiety, alone, can kill you?

Let us talk about anxiety. What is it? According to Merriam-Webster Dictionary, anxiety is an abnormal and overwhelming sense of apprehension and fear. It is often marked by physical signs such as tension, sweating, and increased pulse rate, by doubt concerning the reality and nature of the threat, and by self-doubt about one's capacity to cope with it. That is why God tells us not to worry and, at least 365 times in the Bible, not to fear. 2 Timothy Chapter 1:7 says, "For God has not given us the spirit of fear but of power, and of love, and of a sound mind." In this life's journey, you must keep a sound mind and refrain from self-doubt, stress, worry, and fear.

Whenever you are in a spiritual battle, you must face the enemy, head-on, with power, love, and a sound mind. The Power to know that you are not in this fight alone and that God loves you so much that He wants you to live in a place of peace. No matter how many spirits come against you, do not be afraid of them. Have courage. Know that there is a greater force fighting for you and with you. 1 John 4:4 says, "Ye are of God, little children, and have overcome them: because greater is He that is in you, than he that is in the world."

So, the way to combat fear and anxiety is with *courage*. Well, why not with Peace?" you may ask. Before you can walk in a place of peace, you must first have the boldness to face your fears, conquer them, and walk through them knowing that God is on your side. Once you get to that place in your mindset, then and only then will you enter that place of peace. I am talking about the kind of peace that Christ gives. No one will ever understand you at this point in your life, especially when they can see all the hell and chaos around you.

Remember, it is the peace of Christ that surpasses all understanding, and to obtain it, you must first have courage. Deuteronomy Chapter 31:6, says "Be strong and of good courage, fear not, nor be afraid of them: for the Lord they God, He is that doth go with thee; He will not fail thee or forsake thee. Philippians 4:7, says "And the peace of God, which passeth all understanding, shall keep your hearts and minds through Christ Jesus."

Here is a *bonus* indicator to help you recognize when you are under attack. It is a *Lack of Motivation and Determination*. After all that you have been through, you may ask yourself "Is it worth all of this?" You may find yourself slowing down because you have been worn out in the battle. Sometimes, the battle can be so intense that you, yourself, want to call a cease-fire. Well, that is not up to you. Because you are a child of God, you cannot control the amount of warfare that comes heavily against you, but you can control how long it lasts. Get your motivation and determination back as soon as possible because motivation will help keep you going but determination will help you cross the finish line. What are motivation and determination? Motivation is defined as a motivating force, stimulus, or influence, incentive, or drive. Determination is a firm, or fixed, intention to achieve the desired end.

You must make up in your mind that you are going to do what God has called you to do, whether the devil likes it or not. You must get to a place where you say "It is settled. It is a done deal. It is finished." Jesus said, on the cross at Calvary's mountain, "It is finished." Not that He was finished with us but finished with what He came to do on earth for the world. He had accomplished the mission; the very thing He was sent here to achieve.

Jeremiah Chapter 29, verse 11, says "For I know the thoughts that I think toward you, saith the Lord, thoughts of peace, and not of evil, to give you an expected end." To reach that expected end, you must be motivated as well as determined. Nehemiah was both motivated and determined. The Bible says that Nehemiah faced every challenge, head-on, with courage, wisdom, and determination. One of his greatest motivational speeches was in Chapter 4. He said, in verse 14, to "Remember the Lord who is great and awesome, and fight for your brothers, your sons, your daughters, your wives, and your homes." All these categories, alone, are reasons to fight.

So, the way to combat Lack of Motivation and Determination is to *remember your purpose*. You must remember the reason why God put you here in the first place, and fight for that. You must remember everything and everyone God has entrusted you with and fight for that. Think about what you are still here on this earth to do and fight for that. Most of your attacks are because you have a purpose.

* * *

"God is our refuge and strength, a very present help in trouble. ~Psalm 46:

Seven Ways to Defeat the Enemy

"Wherefore take unto you the whole armour of God, that ye may be able to withstand in the evil day, and having done all, to stand."
~Ephesians 6:13

Now that I have given you four main indicators of under attack, and a bonus one, I want to, now, help you put the pieces together so that it will all make sense. When you are faced with a spiritual battle, or with Spiritual Warfare, God is there to remind you that He is with you. He is with you. He has given you the necessary tools and weapons to stand and face this challenge head-on. He will never leave you to fight it alone. He will never allow you to enter onto any battlefield and not give you anything to fight with. One of the first things you need to do before stepping onto any battlefield, whether it be the battlefield of your mind, your faith, etc., is to make sure you are properly dressed in your battle gear or battle uniform.

When I was in the Marines, we wore a specific type of uniform nearly every day of the week called Cammies, or Utilities. Cammies were The Marine Corps Combat Utility Uniform that we would wear during peaceful times, training times, and, of course, during battle times. One of the purposes for wearing the Cammies during peaceful and training times was so that we would already be prepared and completely dressed in case war broke out, or if we would have to be deployed suddenly. If the enemy were to strike suddenly, we would be dressed and ready to go to battle. Our complete battle uniform, or Cammies, consisted of six major pieces:

YOU ARE UNDER ATTACK

1) *Cammies* – The Marine Corps Combat Utility Uniform or MCCUU. This is the day-to-day utility uniform worn by Marines during normal conditions of peace and abnormal conditions such as training or war.
2) *Cartridge Belt* – A centerpiece used to help hold up Cammies' bottoms and to help carry some of our most important tools needed for the battle which are ammunition, bayonet (knife), and water.
3) *Flak Jacket* – A form of body armor worn to protect the chest, or heart, against stab wounds and bullets. It functions almost like a bulletproof vest.
4) *Combat Boots* – A particular type of lightweight boots to help aid in prolonged standing, walking, or running during battle and so we could tread lightly while approaching enemy territories.
5) *Helmet* – A lightweight helmet user as armor in combat to protect to head, skull, and brain from either bullet wounds, falls, and/or fractures.
6) *Rifle* – To take the enemy out.

Before we can enter on any battlefield, and come out alive, we must first put on our battle gear, or battle uniform. We must put it on and keep it on as much as possible because we never know when the enemy will strike. We must live in it and walk in it daily. Well, what is our battle gear, or battle uniform? I like to call it our A-Gear, which is the Whole Armor of God. This is our spiritual battle uniform, and it also consists of six major pieces, plus a bonus piece to put on before entering the battlefield and to keep on during and after the battle. The bonus piece, or seventh piece, completes the Whole Armor of God; therefore, causing it to be fully effective in our day-to-day lives.

Ephesians Chapter 6:11-13 tells us to put on the whole armour of God, that ye may be able to stand against the wiles of the devil. For we wrestle not against flesh and blood, but against principalities, against powers, against the rulers of the darkness of this world, against spiritual wickedness in high places. Wherefore take unto you the whole armour of God, that ye may be able to withstand in the evil day, and having done all, to stand."

What is the Whole Armor of God exactly? It is a full or complete, spiritual armor given to us by God that will help us fight unforeseen battles. These unforeseen battles are called spiritual battles that transpire from a place of spiritual warfare. The purpose of you putting on the Whole Armor of God and wearing it daily is so that it can provide full natural and spiritual protection while, at the same time, block and redirect whatever was sent to cause you natural or spiritual harm. Even military vehicles are protected in armor so that whenever the enemy strikes at them, they can withstand the force of the enemy's weapons of mass destruction.

Putting on the Full Armor of God is like applying a rule, law, or principle of God to our lives that carries as much weight in a spiritual battle as a fully armored tank in a natural battle. This law, rule, or principle is given to us, from God through the Apostle Paul, to help us successfully stand up against all the wicked schemes, plots, tactics, tricks, and deceit of the devil. This is because the battle that we are fighting is not one of flesh and blood or an opponent that we can physically see. However, it is a battle against a spiritual opponent that we cannot physically see.

My brothers and my sisters, we are fighting against an invisible opponent hidden in rulers, powers, and world forces of this present darkness and against spiritual forces of wickedness in high places. You cannot see him in the natural, but he surely exists in the spiritual. This invisible opponent is none other than the devil, Satan himself.

Now that you have a better overview of the Whole Armor of God and a better understanding of what is going on around you, are ready to fight (stand)? If so, then here are the *seven pieces* of the Whole Armor of God, and the **Seven Ways to Defeat the Enemy**:

1

FIRST WAY TO DEFEAT THE ENEMY

GIRD UP YOUR LOINS WITH TRUTH.

My first way to defeat the enemy is to Gird Up Your Loins with Truth. This is the first piece of the Whole Armor of God. The Truth is one of the most necessary tools you will need before ever stepping on the battlefield. This is because our Bible tells us that God is Truth. Jesus said in John 14:6 "I am the way, the Truth, and the life: no man cometh unto the Father, but by me." The Lord, Himself, is our banner of Truth and there is no question about it. He is the center of our joy and our livelihood. He is the One who helps us keep it all together.

That is just like our belt that we wear every day to help hold up our pants; to help cover and protect the center of our physical stature. It helps cover and protects who we truly are, our gender, our make-up. It helps prevent false identity and helps us face the Truth of our natural being. It also helps keep us protected from the lies and deceptions of Satan, the devil.

Overall, this belt of truth helps us face reality, toughen up, and stand our ground if we must. Meaning it is what it is and there is nothing you can do to change it. Have you ever heard the saying "Pull up your big boy, or girl, pants?" Well, this is when you are ready to fight and face the facts for real.

Regardless of the circumstance, we must always accept the truth, whether it is our own or the reality of what the driving force is behind the things we are going through. I am sure you have been asked this question before: "Do you swear to tell the truth, the whole truth, and nothing but the truth; so, help you, God?" We all have been in that hot seat before. Nevertheless, I believe God placed us in that hot seat, not to shame us, but to set us free. The Bible tells us that "You shall know the Truth and the Truth shall set you free." Turning away from the Truth is one of the worst moves we could ever make in our lives.

When the Jewish leaders wanted Jesus dead, they took Him to Pilate to order His death. Pilate could not find fault in Him and He asked Jesus what Truth was. Jesus never responded because He knew who He was and He knew that, eventually, Truth would speak for itself. If you stay true to who you are where the enemy cannot find fault in you, Truth will eventually speak for you. You will not have to handle your case alone. The Truth will handle it for you. He will also be your defense attorney. The Lord is our Banner of Truth.

Now, before you dress any further in your Armor of God, understand the whole truth behind the warfare in your life and hold on to it. You are a child of God and you have received His son Jesus Christ into your heart.

Anything or anyone, connected to God (Jesus) is bound for an attack. It is inevitable. The day you said "I do" to Christ, the devil aligned his sites on you. You are a target caught in his crossfire and he wants you either dead or alive on his team.

You must remember that Jesus died for you, paid the price for the remission of your sins so that you may have life and life more abundantly. This battle was never meant for you in the first place. This battle is an ongoing, spiritual war between good and evil, between God and Satan. It started before you ever existed, before the beginning of time. It started before God kicked Satan out of Heaven. Ever since then, Satan's payback has been to try to destroy the very thing that God loves the most and that's mankind, who is you.

So, Gird Up Your Loins with Truth by understanding who is really behind the spiritual warfare in your life and, at the same time, keep your integrity(truth) and have the courage to face a battle that you were, somehow, brought in the middle of, even though it is not yours to fight.

2

SECOND WAY TO DEFEAT THE ENEMY

P*UT ON THE BREASTPLATE OF RIGHTEOUSNESS.* My second way to defeat the enemy is to Put on the Breastplate of Righteousness. This is the second piece of the Whole Armor of God. Before we discuss the breastplate, let us first understand Righteousness. What is Righteousness? According to the Merriam-Webster dictionary, righteousness is acting in accord with divine or moral law: free from guilt or sin. It means to come into right standing with God.

How do we come into right standing with God? The only way to come into right standing with God is to make peace with Him. The Word tells us that we are either for Him or against Him, there is no meeting Him halfway. Anyone who is against God becomes an enemy of God. Therefore, the only way Peace can be made with Him is by believing in, accepting, and having faith in Jesus Christ.

Romans 5:1 says, "Therefore, being justified by faith, we have peace with God through our Lord Jesus Christ." Romans 10:4 says, "For Christ is the end of the law for righteousness to every one that believeth." Philippians 3:9 says, "And be found in Him, not having mine own righteousness, which is of the law, but that which is through the faith of Christ, the righteousness which is of God by faith."

When Paul tells us in Ephesians to put on the Breastplate of Righteousness, he is telling us to cover and protect ourselves with Righteousness, Holiness. The dictionary defines a breastplate as a usually metal plate worn as defensive armor for the breast. That word usually means generally, routinely, regularly, often, and even under normal conditions. It is worn to protect the chest from fatal wounds. Why is it so important to protect the chest? Because one of our main organs for living is in the chest and that is our heart.

In combat training, the first place the Marine is taught to align the sites of their weapon is at center mass. We know that the heart is the most vital organ in all living beings. It is also at the heart of the matter, or the root of the issue, where we will find the source of many of our problems. Once you get to the heart of the matter, then the issue can be resolved. This is what Satan wants from you so badly that he is willing to do any and everything to get it. It is your spiritual heart. The devil knows that if he can get to your spiritual heart, which is the vital source and center of who you are, then your heart will send signals to your mind (soul); therefore, telling your flesh (body) how it ought to respond.

So, we must Put on the Breastplate of Righteousness because Righteousness is the mirror reflection of the complete Armor of God. Wearing it every day of our lives helps keep our hearts covered and protected from any and everything the enemy sends our way. If we are not protected with the Breastplate of Righteousness, our spiritual hearts are left exposed to the deceitful attacks of the enemy. When our hearts deceive us, it is easy to sin and fall short of the Glory of God.

3

THIRD WAY TO DEFEAT THE ENEMY

***S**HOD YOUR FEET WITH THE GOSPEL OF PEACE.* My third way to defeat the enemy is to Shod Your Feet with the Preparation of the Gospel of Peace. This is the third piece of the Whole Armor of God. The word Shod means shoe, in the past tense. It simplifies the wearing of footwear or shoes. The Amplified Bible version of this scripture says "And having strapped on your feet the Gospel of peace in preparation [to face the enemy with firm-footed stability and the readiness produced by the good news.] (Amp). This means to stand firm in what God has called you to do and be ready to face whatever attack comes your way because of spreading the Good News of Jesus Christ.

Find peace in knowing that Satan awaits you at the door, ready to attack and knock you down so you will not go where God has told you to go, you will not do what God has told you to, or you will not become who God has called you to become. God has already gone before you and has made your path straight. Be okay with knowing that many spirits will come against you. You will be talked about, ridiculed, judged, and persecuted all for His name's sake. But if God is for you, then who can be against you? Greater is He that is in you than he that is in the world!

So, you must Shod Your Feet with the Preparation of the Gospel of Peace and make up in your mind that you are ready to stand your ground, face your fears and do whatever God has placed you on this earth to do, without fear or anxiety. For God has not given you the spirit of fear but of power, love, and a sound mind. My brothers and my sisters, God has given us the Peace and confidence to let our lights shine in all the earth and to go and spread the Good News, which is the Gospel of Jesus Christ. Are you ready?

4

FOURTH WAY TO DEFEAT THE ENEMY

LIFT UP THE SHIELD OF FAITH. My fourth way to defeat the enemy is to Lift Up the Shield of Faith. This is the fourth piece of the Whole Armor of God. What is a shield? According to en.wikipedia.org, a shield is a piece of personal armor held in the hand, which may or may not be strapped to the wrist or forearm. Shields are used to intercepting specific attacks as well as to protect while in combat.

They were also used in the earlier times by Roman Soldiers.

Spiritually, shields are used to block the attacks of the enemy and to quench his fiery darts. Well, in this case, your spiritual shield is faith. You must protect yourself, and even those around you, by lifting your shield of faith.

Now, let us deal with Faith. We know that faith is the substance of things hoped for and the evidence of things unseen. How can we apply this principle to things unseen? How can we apply this principle of faith by believing in and trusting in a God that we cannot see with the natural eye? We believe that He exists, that He is real, and we trust that He will watch over and protect us every day of our lives.

You may also ask "How can one lift faith as a shield?" Whenever you are in battle, or under attack, you must lift your faith as a protective shield by simply raising it and holding on to it. There will be times when it does not look like God is going to come through for you neither does it look like you are going to make it out of this battle alive. This is where you should put your faith to work. This is where you must increase it, hold on to it and never lose it.

If a shield is something that may or may not be attached to the wrist or forearm, then that means you may or may not lose it in battle. If it is attached, you have a better chance of it being protective than you would if it were not attached. You have the choice of whether you will hold on to it or risk losing it. The same as faith.

Remember, you can always lose what is not properly attached. Therefore, your faith cannot be loosely handled in the time of war. As you hold on to your faith, it gives you the confidence of knowing that God is right there in the battle fighting for you and with you. Having faith and knowing that God is with you, allows you to fight from a position of peace. Peace gives you hope that everything will be alright and that you will come out of this battle alive. Not only will you come out alive, but you will also come out alive and victorious.

You remember reciting the 23rd Psalm when you were a kid growing up: "Yea though I walk through the valley of the shadow of death, I will fear no evil: for thou art with me; thy rod and thy staff, they comfort me."

Well, now is not the time to only recite the 23rd Psalm when you are under attack. When you are under attack, it is now time to believe the 23rd Psalm and put your faith into action.

James Chapter 2, verse 17, says that "Even so faith, if it hath not works is dead, being alone." Believing that God is real and that He will fight your battles is great but knowing that God is real and that He will fight your battles is even greater. Satan also believes in God. He knows that God is real; that is why he trembles at just the mention of His name. Abraham believed in God, but he put his faith into action when he offered his son, Isaac, upon the altar as a sacrifice to the Lord. With Abraham's faith came his works and by his works was his faith made perfect. Your faith is made perfect when you believe and act.

So, above all, *Lift the Shield of Faith* with which you can extinguish (quench; end; reduce its effectiveness; nullify) all the flaming arrows of the devil and be protected in this battle. Above all the other pieces of the Whole Armor of God, your faith in the time of battle is the most important weapon. None of the other pieces will benefit you if you do not have faith. You must believe that it works. This is one reason why God gave each of us a measure of faith, according to Romans 12:3. With your measure of Faith, remain steadfast, secured, rooted, and grounded; knowing that God will never leave you nor forsake you. He will work it all out in your favor and will always bring you out on the other side.

5

FIFTH WAY TO DEFEAT THE ENEMY

T*AKE THE HELMET OF SALVATION.* My fifth way to defeat the enemy is to Take the Helmet of Salvation. This is the fifth piece of the Whole Armor of God. A Helmet is a covering, or enclosed headpiece, of ancient or medieval armor. It is a protective head covering usually made of hard material to resist Impact. It is one of the most important pieces during times of battle. With it being the fifth piece of armor, it is probably the last piece many of us put on but should always be the first one that we pick up. That is just like going for a ride on a motorcycle. The helmet is one of the first, most important, pieces needed but is normally the last piece grabbed before heading out the door. Well, thank God for His grace!

Spiritually, the number five represents grace and before we can understand why Apostle Paul related the Helmet to Salvation, we must first understand grace. Grace is God's unmerited and undeserved favor. It was because of His grace that we were ever given a chance at Salvation. What is Salvation? From a Christian standpoint, the Bible defines Salvation as being saved through grace from the penalty of sin.

Ephesians 2:8 tells us that "For by grace are ye saved through faith, and that not of yourselves: it is the gift of God." Romans 5:8-10 says, "But God commendeth His love toward us, in that while we were yet sinners, Christ died for us. Much more then, being now justified by His blood, we shall be saved from wrath through Him. For if, when we were enemies, we were reconciled to God by the death of His Son, much more being reconciled, we shall be saved by His life. "So, Salvation is God's arms opened wide, waiting to accept us and to adopt us into His family through the bloodshed of His precious Son, Jesus Christ.

Why did Apostle Paul relate the Helmet to Salvation? The natural Helmet protects soldiers from fatal wounds to the brain in a natural battle, therefore, the spiritual helmet protects Christian soldiers from fatal wounds to the mind in a spiritual battle. Again, the first place the enemy tries to attack in any situation of life is the mind. The enemy will fight you for your mind because he wants to take away your salvation.

I stated earlier that the mind is the battlefield. It is a stomping ground for the devil. Satan loves to send fatal, discouraging, and evil thoughts to your mind in hopes to shift or kill the Christian side of you. He knows that if he can get through to your mind, then he has access to every other part of your spiritual being.

Have you ever felt like you were losing it and that your mind was messing with you?" Well, I am here to tell you that, as a child of God, you are not losing it and your mind is not messing with you. You are not crazy!

Your mind cannot mess with you, but Satan can and is. It is not you, but it is the evil one whom we call the devil. You must protect your mind (your thoughts) with *The Helmet of Salvation* because your salvation is what he is after. Never let the devil intimidate you, corrupt you, or, most importantly, challenge or change your mind. So, hold fast to your salvation and your love for Jesus Christ and know that this battle is not yours, it is the Lords.

6

SIXTH WAY TO DEFEAT THE ENEMY

T*AKE THE SWORD OF THE SPIRIT.* My sixth way to defeat the enemy is to *Take Up the Sword of the Spirit.* This is the sixth piece of the Whole Armor of God. A sword also called a gladius, is a weapon with a long blade used for cutting, thrusting, or striking. According to en.wikipedia.org, Gladius is a Latin word meaning "sword" that was used by Ancient Roman foot soldiers. Most foot soldiers would protect themselves behind a shield, but they would strike the enemy with the gladius.

Often, the sword has also been used as a symbol of honor, or authority. We know that wherever there is an honor, there is, in most cases, authority. Likewise, wherever there is authority, there is either influence or fear. In combat, the sword was present, hopefully, to bring fear upon the enemy as well as take the enemy out. If ever used correctly, it can cut through, cut off, and cut down the strongest opponent. When it is handled properly by a true soldier, it can do great damage to the enemy.

When I was in the Marines, we were each issued an M16 Rifle, 9MM Pistol, and Bayonet Knife. We wore the Bayonet on our cartridge belt, around our waist, in case there were times when close combat was necessary. The Bayonet was about 12 inches in length altogether but had a blade that was about seven inches long.

Just like a Bayonet was given to military soldiers and a gladius given to Roman Soldiers, a sword was given to

God's soldiers. This sword is the Sword of the Spirit, which is The Word of God. All the other pieces of the Whole Armor of God are there to keep us covered, but the Word of God is there to keep us alive. The Word is our most powerful weapon against the enemy. When used properly, the Word can take the devil out.

How can we use The Word of God as The Sword of the Spirit? Since the sword, just like the M16 rifle, is used to take out the enemy in the natural, The Word of God is used to take out the enemy in the spiritual. The devil is a spirit, and you cannot fight spirit with carnal, or natural, weapons. You must fight spirit to spirit using spiritual weapons. In other words, you must use God's powerful words against the devil by 1) writing His scriptures, 2) reading them, 3) studying them, and 4) reciting them out loud. If the Word is used correctly, it can pierce through, cut off, and shoot down the attacks of the evil one. Hebrews Chapter 4, verse 12, says "For the Word of God is quick, and powerful, and sharper than any two-edged sword, piercing even to the dividing asunder of soul and spirit, and the joints and marrow, and is a discerner of the thoughts and intents of the heart."

Remember, there will always be times when Satan will

try to attack you with his words. You will not be able to see him naturally, but you will be able to hear him spiritually. He comes at you, disguised, in words from people, whether spoken or written. He comes at you disguised in negative doctor reports. He also comes at you, disguised, in words or thoughts in your very own mind. Regardless, he uses words to attack you so you must use words, God's words, to fight him back. Your words are powerless, but God's words are powerful.

When Jesus was led into the wilderness by the Spirit, He was tempted by Satan with words. The word 'Spirit' has a capital S. That shows that Jesus was led in the wilderness by God, the Father. Sometimes, God will allow us to be tempted by the words of the enemy to test us and see how we will respond. Jesus' response to the words of Satan was the words of His Father, God. Each time He was attacked with words, He responded with "It is written." He then quoted the Word of God by scripture. He fought back with the Sword of the Spirit, the Word of God.

It was not that Jesus could not handle Satan. He's God. Of course, He could. It was the fact that He was God in the flesh, and He was at one of the weakest times in His natural life. The Bible tells us that it was after He had fasted for 40 days and 40 nights that He hungered. The enemy will always attack you at your weakest moment in life. The good news is that when you are at your weakest moments, it is the best time for God to demonstrate His strength and power through His Word.

The Word tells us, in 2 Corinthians 12:9, that our strength is made perfect in weakness. Paul said, "I rather glory in my infirmities, so that the power of Christ may rest upon me." He said, "Therefore I take pleasure in infirmities, in reproaches, in necessities, in persecutions, in distresses for Christ's sake: for when I am weak, then I am strong." You are strong in your weakest moments because God's Word is standing strong in you.

So, how are you strengthened in times of weakness? Through the Word of God. Read it. Hear it. Speak it and apply it to your life. Use it as your weapon against the enemy. Take Up the Sword of the Spirit and fight the devil back. Arm yourself, always, with the powerful Word of God.

7

SEVENTH WAY TO DEFEAT THE ENEMY

P**RAY.** My seventh and final way to defeat the enemy is through Prayer. This is the seventh and complete piece of the Whole Armor of God. Without Prayer, your armor is not complete, and you are not fully equipped for battle. A lot of times, we stop at the sixth piece, forgetting that prayer is also a part of this uniform. We fail to realize how important it is in our lives. All the other pieces of the armor are not fully effective without this final piece.

Prayer brings us closer to God and keeps us in His presence. It helps us to hear God and obtain battle strategies from Him. Without His presence and strategies for our lives, especially during times of battle, we have no strength, wisdom, or power. Without strength, wisdom, and power, we cannot fight.

Have you ever seen a soldier on a battlefield all armored down but have no weapon to fight with? Yes, you can fight with a sword in the natural, but you cannot fight with a sword in the spiritual unless it is the Word of God. Utilizing the Word of God in prayer is like cutting off the enemy's head. It is like having ammunition in your rifle. Yes, the rifle is a powerful weapon, but it is more effective with ammunition. Likewise, the Word of God is also a powerful weapon and is more effective with a prayer life. Your rifle needs ammunition, and your ammunition needs a rifle. The Word of God is powerful alone, but you also need prayer in your life to win the battle. One cannot function properly without the other. When both are working together, then you have a weapon of mass destruction. When they are effectively used together, then, and only then are you aiming your weapon at your true enemy, Satan.

Praying God's Word over your life during times of battle shows God how much you need Him and are depending on Him to survive. This touches God's heart and causes Him to react on your behalf. I depend on God so much that my whole life is centered around prayer. Each morning when I open my eyes, I immediately say a prayer. As soon as my feet touch the floor, I get down on my knees and say another prayer.

I thank God for allowing my children and me to see another day. I thank Him for watching over my family as we slept all night long. I thank Him for being our security and our protection. I ask Him to go before us in our day and remove stumbling blocks. Clear our pathways from all hurt, harm, and danger. I ask Him to cover us as we leave our home and bring us back safe and sound, and on time at the end of the day. This is just my daily prayer.

Even during the day, we still must steal away from our tasks, or chores, and pray. If we do not feel the need to pray for ourselves, then we can pray for somebody else. There is always someone out there who is going through similar warfare as you. They may not be as strong in their faith as you and they could use your help. You can help them by praying for them. You can help them by praying for their loved ones. You can help them by praying for this world around them.

At the end of my day, I say another prayer before going to bed. I am not talking about the common prayer that many of us have prayed when we were little:

"Now I lay me down to sleep, I pray the Lord my soul to keep. If I should die before I wake, I pray the Lord my soul to take."

Although that is still a powerful prayer, it was good for us when we were little. Now it is time to take it up a notch. Do not wait until you are going through something to pray. Go ahead and increase your prayer life now. So, when the enemy comes at you with a blow, you are trained in prayer and can strike him back with a blow. Dying before your time is not an option for you. You shall live and not die and declare the works of the Lord, according to Psalm Chapter 118, verse 17.

So, get in position. Man your battle station. Arm and posture yourself in prayer and get ready to pray the Word of God. Look beyond everything and everyone that is causing you problems in the natural. Make sure you are locked and loaded and aim your weapon (prayers) at the true enemy, Satan. Now that you are locked and loaded and in the proper position, Ready, Aim, Fire! Pray and pray without ceasing. Your prayers, and the prayers of others, can defeat the enemy and help save your life.

What shall we then say to these things? If God be for us, who can be against us? ~Romans 8:3

"Ye are of God, little children, and have overcome them: because greater is He that is in you, than he that is in the world.
~1 John 4:4

"I returned, and saw under the sun, that the race is not to the swift, nor the battle to the strong, neither yet bread to the wise, nor yet riches to men of understanding, nor yet favour to men of skill; but time and chance happeneth to them all."
~Ecclesiastes 9:11

"But he that shall endure unto the end, the same shall be saved." ~Matthew 24:13

Conclusion

"These things I have spoken unto you, that in me ye might have peace. In the world ye shall have tribulation: but be of good cheer; I have overcome the world."
~John 16:33

I pray that something was written in this book to encourage you and help you along your way. Just remember, as you continue your journey throughout life, the enemy will always try to attack you in some form or another. Whether it is through people, relationships, finances, health, or even your mind, fight him back with the spiritual weapons God has given you.

Again, your seven spiritual weapons to defeat the enemy are 1) The Belt of Truth, 2) The Breastplate of Righteousness, 3) The Preparation of the Gospel of Peace, 4) The Shield of Faith, 5) The Helmet of Salvation, 6) The Sword of the Spirit, which is the Word of God, and 7) Prayer.

If you are suited in the Whole Armor of God, you are protected. If you use your spiritual weapons properly, you will come out victorious. Do not allow the enemy to take you down without a fight. Use your weapons and fight until this battle is over. God gave them to you and placed them in your hands for this very reason. Now it is up to you to use them.

"The only way for you not to make it on this journey is for you to stop. Do not give up. Keep going."
~Sabrina D. Thorps

Prayer of Thanksgiving

"He that dwelleth in the secret place of the Most High shall abide under the shadow of the Almighty. I will say of the Lord, He is my refuge and my fortress, my God, in Him will I trust."
~Psalm 91:1-2

Dear Lord, we come together in unity, thanking you for the Whole Armor of God. Thank you for giving us the spiritual weapons needed to fight against the enemy. Thank you for the Belt of Truth to protect us from the lies, deceptions, and evil thoughts from the enemy. Thank you for the Breastplate of

Righteousness to cover and protect our hearts so that we may live a holy lifestyle. Thank you for the Shoes of the Gospel of Peace to help us walk in spiritual boldness; ready to share your word wherever we go. Thank you for the Shield of Faith to block every arrow and extinguish every fiery dart thrown at us from the enemy. To give us hope and confidence that you are always with us. You will never leave us nor forsake us.

Lord, we thank you for the Sword of the Spirit, the Word of God, to use in battle. To pull down strongholds, break chains in the spiritual realm, and set our minds free from bondage and captivity.

Thank you for giving us a Prayer life where we can experience your divine presence. Letting us know that you are with us in battle and that you are fighting on our side. Most of all, Lord, we thank you for the Helmet of Salvation to cover and protect our minds from negative words and evil thoughts. To wear as a crown and an honor that we are saved, by grace, from the hands of the enemy. Our sins have been forgiven and sleight has been washed clean by the blood of Jesus. That You paid the ultimate price for our sins so that we would not have to.

So that we may have life and life more abundantly.
Amen.

About the Author

Sabrina D. Thorps was born in Meridian, Mississippi, and raised in a small place called Lisman, Alabama. She graduated from Choctaw County High School in

Butler, Alabama. From there, she went on to graduate from Marine Corps Boot Camp Paris Island, SC and became one of The Few, The Proud, The Marines.

Sabrina began her book-writing journey around the age of 10 when she was in fifth grade. She wrote many stories and books, but never published them because it was never about the money for her. She realized that she had been given a gift to write and she wanted to use that gift to reach people around the world.

In 2017, when Sabrina first realized that she was in Spiritual Warfare, she heard God whisper the words "You Are Under Attack." She knew then that what she was going through and the enemy she was facing could not be seen with the naked eye. She knew that it was an enemy that could only be dealt with in the spiritual realm.

After going through this trying time in her life, Sabrina realized that this was another area of her calling where God wanted to use her. One of her assignments in the military was to teach and train Marines on how to defeat the enemy with the M-16 Rifle and 9MM Pistol. She now believes that God has given her a passion to do the same in His Kingdom but from a more spiritual standpoint. In this book, Sabrina helps God's people recognize when they are being attacked by the devil and how to defeat him through the Word of God.

www.SabrinaThorps.com

Thanks for reading! Please add a short review on Amazon and let me know what you thought!

For more books by Sabrina D. Thorps and general information, please visit her website at **www.SabrinaThorps.com**.

For book publishing information, please visit: **www.dreamwisepublishing.com**.

To follow Sabrina on Facebook, please visit **www.facebook.com/sabrinadthorps**.

To follow her on Instagram, please visit @sabrinathorpsministries.

Thanks, and keep fighting the good fight of **FAITH**.
I Love You All

Notes

Merriam-Webster Online, "Warfare," Merriam-Webster Dictionary, https://www.merriam-webster.com/dictionary/warfare (accessed April 12, 2021).

Wikipedia The Free Encyclopedia, "Spiritual Warfare," https://en.wikipedia.org/wiki/Spiritualwarfare (accessed April 12, 2021).

Merriam-Webster Online, "Anxiety," Merriam-Webster Dictionary, https://www.merriam-webster.com/dictionary/anxiety (accessed April 12, 2021).

Merriam-Webster Online, "Motivation," Merriam-Webster Dictionary, https://www.merriam-webster.com/dictionary/motivation (accessed April 12, 2021).

Merriam-Webster Online, "Determination," Merriam-Webster Dictionary, https://www.merriam-webster.com/dictionary/determination (accessed April 12, 2021).

Merriam-Webster Online, "Righteousness," Merriam-Webster Dictionary, https://www.merriam-webster.com/dictionary/righteousness (accessed April 12, 2021).

Merriam-Webster Online, "Shod," Merriam-Webster Dictionary, https://www.merriam-webster.com/dictionary/shod (accessed April 12, 2021).

Merriam-Webster Online, "Shield," Merriam-Webster Dictionary, https://www.merriam-webster.com/dictionary/shield (accessed April 12, 2021).

Merriam-Webster Online, "Sword," Merriam-Webster Dictionary, https://www.merriam-webster.com/dictionary/sword (accessed April 12, 2021).

Wikipedia The Free Encyclopedia, "Cammies," https://en.wikipedia.org/wiki/cammies (accessed April 12, 2021).

Wikipedia The Free Encyclopedia, "Flat Jacket," https://en.wikipedia.org/wiki/flatjacket (accessed April 12, 2021).

Wikipedia The Free Encyclopedia, "Gladius," https://en.wikipedia.org/wiki/gladius (accessed April 12, 2021).

YOU ARE UNDER ATTACK

YOU ARE UNDER ATTACK

YOU ARE UNDER ATTACK

YOU ARE UNDER ATTACK